The SARI-SARI STORE

A Philippine Scrapbook

Compiled by
Rebecca C. Asedillo and B. David Williams

ƒ

FRIENDSHIP PRESS
NEW YORK

Library of Congress Cataloging-in-Publication Data
Asedillo, Rebecca C., 1950-
　The sari-sari store.

　1. Philippines—Civilization. I. Williams, B. David. II. Title.
DS664.A84　　1989　　959.9　　88-33423
ISBN 0-377-00195-3

Drawings by Orlando Castillo on pages 39, 41, 55 and 61 are for the benefit of Likha Promotions, a national cultural network promoting Philippine art and heritage to North American audiences. Likha National Secretarial (415) 534-3769. With special thanks to the generous support of the Philippine Education Support Committee.

ISBN 0-377-00195-3

Editorial Offices: 475 Riverside Drive, Room 772, New York, NY 10115
Distribution Offices: P.O. Box 37844, Cincinnati, OH 45222-0844
Copyright © 1989 Friendship Press, Inc.
Printed in the United States of America

TABLE OF CONTENTS

1. FOLKTALES OF ANCIENT ISLANDS
The Origin of the Rainbow, 1; Makisig, the Little Hero of Mactan, 2; A Maguindanao Version of the Radia Indarapatra Folk Epic, 6

2. THE SPANISH ARRIVE
Mindanao, 8; The Speed of the *Barangay,* 9

3. HEROES OF A NATION
José Rizal, 11; Andres Bonifacio, 18

4. IN DEFENSE OF FREEDOM
President Emilio Aguinaldo Addresses the Filipino People, 21; Senator Alfred J. Beveridge Addresses the U.S. Senate, 23; Other Voices, 25; All, of Whatever Race or Color, Are Entitled to Life, Liberty and the Pursuit of Happiness, 27; We Are a World Power, 27; Letters from the Philippines, 28

5. TOWARD A SOVEREIGN NATION
The Philippine National Anthem, 31; The Philippine Flag, 34

6. IMAGES FROM PROTESTANT MISSION
Staunton of Sagada, 35; Selections from Missionary Letters, 38

7. THE STRUGGLE CONTINUES
For Father Romano on His 45th Birthday, 42; An Agape Celebration, 44; Who Am I? 47; P.B., 48; The Immortal Words of Macli-ing, 50

8. A RICH AND GRACEFUL CULTURE
From the Writings of Carlos Bulosan, 51; Postnatal Care, 53; Recipes from the Philippines, 56; Games from the Philippines, 61; Some Tagalog Proverbs, 72; A Philippine Quiz, 73; Some Filipino Riddles, 74

1.
FOLKTALES OF ANCIENT ISLANDS

The Origin of the Rainbow

In the early days of the world, it is said that there was no rainbow. This beautiful multi-colored arc that stretches from the earth to the sky was first used by Bathala, supreme lord of the sky and king of the gods and goddesses, as a bridge to connect the earth and heaven.

In those days, Bathala and the lesser gods and goddesses used to live on earth with the people. They taught the people how to hunt for food in the forest, how to raise food from the earth, how to make war, and how to cure illnesses.

One day, Bathala decided to visit his kingdom in the sky. He ordered to be brought to him his strong fine horse, which could jump over the mountains and could run as fast as the wind. Bathala's servants immediately mounted on its back the most beautiful saddle, made of fine leather and decorated with silver and gold. Bathala then informed his people where he was going and bade them all good-bye.

Bathala and his horse travelled to the end of the earth until they reached a vast ocean. This was the most extreme point of the earth and had to be crossed in going to the sky. This place was also the nearest to the sky and on clear days one could hear the voices of the sky-people.

Bathala stopped his horse and in a loud voice called to his servants in the sky, ordering them to place a bridge so that he could pass through. Suddenly, a beautiful multi-colored bridge appeared in the sky, brightening Bathala's pathway.

Bathala's servants lowered one end of the bridge until it connected the earth to the sky. Over this heavenly bridge Bathala spurred his horse, reaching heaven without further delay.

Since that time the rainbow has been called *baha hari* or pathbridge of the king. Today, when people see the rainbow, they know that Bathala is again on his powerful horse, journeying from the earth to the sky, to visit his kingdom there.

Adapted from a Tagalog folktale by Teresita Veloso Pil, in *Philippine Folk Fiction and Tales*, Quezon City: New Day Publishers, 1977.

Makisig, the Little Hero of Mactan

This award-winning children's story is based on the fall of Magellan on the island of Cebu in 1521.

Hundreds of years ago, on the island of Mactan there lived a boy called Makisig.

He lived with his father and mother in a small nipa house built near the shore of the sea.

They were part of the barangay ruled by a powerful and good datu by the name of Lapu-Lapu.

One cool morning, Makisig woke up when the sky was still powdered with pale stars. His parents were sound asleep.

An idea came to his mind: he would go to the river, catch fish for their breakfast and surprise his parents. How pleased they would be! And what fun he would have sailing their colorful *birey* all by himself! It was such a swift small boat that Makisig anticipated much excitement.

He got to his feet quietly and picked up his clothes, crept out of the house and went down to the sea. The water was very cold. He bathed himself and dressed hurriedly.

Then he got into the *birey* which was tied near the shore.

The tide was low and only a gentle breeze blew. Makisig had to paddle a longer way than usual to catch fish. When he came to a good spot, he cast his net.

While he waited for the net to fill, he watched the rising sun slowly covering the sky with a brilliant orange glow.

As he gazed at the endless stretch of water before him, he wondered about the other lands beyond Mactan. He had often asked himself the same question when he saw the boats of Chinese traders.

Suddenly, Makisig saw something very strange—a white flapping thing. It was so far away that he could not figure out what it was.

Could it be an *aswang*? Or perhaps a *mananangal* in white robes? It was coming nearer all the time and Makisig grew frightened.

Makisig kept on watching. Soon, he saw more white things flapping.

Then he saw a large brown object, under the white. A boat! So different and so huge! It was many times larger than his *birey*. It was even bigger than the Chinese junks and war boats of Mactan!

Then Makisig was frightened—strange white men were running about the boat. They were pointing at the land, shouting in a language he could not understand.

E. D. Rodriguez

Makisig hastily pulled up his net and paddled with all his might. He must tell the datu about these strange men and their monstrous boat.

When he reached the shore Makisig raced past his own house. He cried, "Father, wake up! Wake up! There are strange white men coming!"

He shouted the same warning as he ran past the houses of the warriors of Mactan. Then he ran on to the palace of Datu Lapu-Lapu.

Finally, he reached the palace. But the warriors guarding the datu would not let Makisig in.

"The datu is still asleep," they said and they crossed their spears to keep Makisig out.

"But there are strange-looking men with boats far larger than ours out there!" Makisig cried.

As the warriors looked toward the sea, Makisig dashed under their crossed spears, through the gates, and into the palace.

Datu Lapu-Lapu listened to Makisig and then ordered a guard to sound a brass gong to call all his men.

The warriors came quickly. They had their wooden shields, deadly spears, poison-tipped arrows and sharp daggers. They rushed to the shore to meet the strangers.

Makisig followed closely. Near the shore he climbed a coconut tree.

From his perch Makisig saw that the strange boats had anchored where the water was deep. The white men lowered small boats and rowed them toward the shore.

Then a fierce battle began. Magellan's men and the warriors of Mactan clashed furiously. Many of the warriors were killed.

They could not hit the white men because they wore suits of metal which gleamed in the sun. Soon the water was red with the blood of the warriors.

Then the white men set fire to the houses. Makisig could hardly see what was happening because of the smoke.

"Aim low at their uncovered legs!" Lapu-Lapu commanded his warriors.

And one by one the white men fell.

Datu Lapu-Lapu finally struck Magellan down.

When they saw their leader dead, the white men rushed back to their boats and finally sailed out of sight. The people of Mactan were victorious.

Makisig climbed down from the tree and ran to his father, who had fought bravely beside the datu.

Then Datu Lapu-Lapu called Makisig. He put a weary hand on the little boy's head and said, "Makisig, you are the bravest warrior in all Mactan. By your warning, you saved your land and people from invaders. You shall be rewarded."

Makisig looked up at the great Lapu-Lapu. He felt he needed nothing more than the good datu's praise to make him proud and happy.

From Cruz, Gemma. *Makisig, The Little Hero of Mactan*. Makati, Philippines: Pamana, Inc., 1964. Used with the author's permission.

A Maguindanao Version of the Radia Indarapatra Folk Epic

The Maguindanao people are one of the major Muslim groups on the island of Mindanao.

O Hinagud!
O great spear
Of hardened, holy wood
With point of blessed metal,
Go you high!
Go far!
Meet you the magic of my foes;
Strike you the magic
Of mine enemies,
Take your blows,
And strike again!
Strike surely — swiftly,
Unrelentingly.
In God's name I thus entreat;
With God's voice
I thus command you;
I, the Emperor,
The King,
Indarapatra.

Far above the sunset clouds,
In an arc of flaming splendor,
Hinagud cleft the sky,
And fell upon the summit
Of angry Bud Matutun;
And the thunder crashed
And rumbled
Through the sullen hills.
And the mighty mountain split,
Throwing high a horrid vomit
Of burning rocks.
And the tortured land
Rocked and trembled.

So great Indarapartra lived in state,
And taught the simple arts
Of farm and field.

He taught the huntsman's tricks,
The herdmen's lore;
He taught the fisher-folk
To call the winds.
He taught the use of iron;
How to make the *kris*,
The long sword, and *barung*,
He taught the farmer
Better ways to sow
And reap;
The women how to weave,
He showed them healing herbs;
Made potions for their easements.
And magic charms
To save them from the Gods
And *Daimons* of the depths.

Translated by Frank L. Minton, and quoted in Del Castillo and Medina. *Philippine Literature from Ancient Times to the Present,* as presented in Gowing, Peter G., *Muslim Filipinos— Heritage and Horizon,* Quezon City: New Day Publishers, 1979.

2.
THE SPANISH ARRIVE

Mindanao

This first-known Western description of Mindanao was made in about 1554 by the Italian pilot Giovanni Gaetano, of the Spanish ship San Juan.

This island is very large: after circumnavigating it we found that it was 2,200 kilometers around, and extends mainly east and west; its highest latitude will be in 11° 30', the lowest in 5° or 6°. It is inhabited by many and varied people: there are Moros, gentiles, and different kings and lords who wear certain clothes without sleeves, short, like marlottas, which they call *patolas*, and the rich have them of silk like taffeta, and the other people of cotton and in different styles. They have many offensive arms of iron and steel, such as scimitars, daggers and spears; and defensive arms they make of animal hide, which is tougher and stronger than that of anta. In a certain part of the island which the Moros rule over, there is small artillery. There are pigs, deer and buffalos in that island, and other animals of the chase and Castilian chickens, and rice and palms and coconuts. There is no corn in it, but they use rice for bread, and a bark which they call *sagu*, from which oil is extracted as from palms and they make bread of it in that land. There is very special gold, which is dug out of mines in the same land; they value it, and use it for exchange, and wear chains and jewelry made of it. On the headland of this island on the west, there is much cinnamon, and the Portuguese touch there when they go to the Moluccas.

From Giovanni B. Ramusio, *Delle Navigationi et Viaggi*, (Venice, 1554, 2nd ed.) Vol. 1, fol. 375- v, as presented in Scott, William Henry, *Cracks in the Parchment Curtain*, Quezon City: New Day Publishers, 1982.

The Speed of the *Barangay*

Let us say something about the speed of these ancient boats of the Visayans, which was certainly great in a *barangay* of one *encomendero* of these islands called Pedro Mendez, which—though I did not see it, I heard about it from many who embarked on it many times—was so fast that nobody in it could keep his footing when they were rowing; even though it had no more than two banks of paddlers, one on each side, it was of low freeboard and long, so they struck the water well with their paddles. It used to travel by paddling between sunrise and sunset from the town of Paranas—where many of these *barangays* are made, and the same Filipino expert who made them made me a little one—to the City of Cebu, where the said Pedro Mendez had his house, this being a distance of more than forty leagues between leaving the one town as the sun was rising and reaching the other before it set, which seems unbelievable since they were traveling at more than four leagues an hour, but the number of witnesses leaves no room for doubt. And I experienced practically the same thing in this little *barangay* which was made in the same town, for I never met another boat and made *romba*—which is what the Filipinos call *recateado* in Spain, which for those who do not know it, is to race—that could keep up with me, and oftentimes when I was sailing near the edge of the sea or some river, I noticed that no man could keep up with me no matter how long he ran along the beach following me.

Description by Fr. Francisco Alcina, *Historia de las Islas e Indios de las Bisayas*, MS 1668, cap. 10, as presented in Scott, William Henry. *Cracks in the Parchment Curtain*, Quezon City: New Day Publishers, 1982.

A Roman Catholic church in the province of La Unión.

3.
HEROES OF A NATION

José Rizal

While virtually all other Filipino national heroes seem subject to controversy, José Rizal is universally admired and considered *the* national hero. Evidence of this is seen nearly everywhere in the Philippines. Statues of Rizal are found in countless town plazas. His picture hangs in many classrooms. He appears on the two peso bill, the one peso coin, and on postage stamps. Main streets across the nation are named "Rizal Street" or "Rizal Avenue." An entire province carries his name. Theatres, parks, cement, matches and cigars have been named after him! An organization called the Knights of Rizal, with chapters in the Philippines and in foreign countries, is dedicated to perpetuating his teachings. Many volumes have been written about Rizal. His birthday, June 19, and the day he was martyred, December 30, are national holidays.

Some have called José Rizal "the New Filipino," feeling that he represented the flowering of the Filipino's highest aspirations during the Spanish period. He was born in 1861, in Calamba, Laguna, of parents belonging to the local elite and having a touch of Chinese ancestry. His family valued education highly and had a substantial library—unusual in days when the authorities tried to limit the availability of books to Filipinos. Rizal was apparently a precocious, sensitive child. While quite young he was left with a lifelong impression of the Spanish authorities' roughness and injustice when his mother was intimidated into confessing guilt of a crime she had not committed. She was later absolved, but the impression had been made.

Rizal was an outstanding student, attending Ateneo de Manila and the University of Santo Tomas, where he studied medicine, philosophy and literature and won literary awards. He went to Spain and enrolled in the Universidad de Madrid, specializing in opthalmic surgery. It was not unusual at that time for the sons of *ilustrados* to go to Europe to study, particularly those in danger at home because of their nationalistic views. Upon the completion of his degree, Rizal served as assistant under two eminent opthalmic surgeons, Louis de Wecker in Paris and Otto Decker in Heidelberg. He learned several European languages well.

While in Europe, Rizal joined an organization of Filipino students called the Propaganda Movement. In Berlin, at the age of twenty-six, he wrote his first novel, *Noli Me Tangere* ("Do Not Touch Me"), which carried a powerful socio-political message. He wrote a second novel, *El Filibusterismo* (usually translated "The Subversive"). These are widely available in a number of languages and are considered to be not only of important social value, but of high literary quality. The Spanish clergy in the Philippines found both novels offensive, and they were banned. The Dominicans charged that *Noli Me Tangere* was "heretical, impious and scandalous from the religious perspective, antipatriotic and subversive from the political point of view, injurious to the Spanish government...."

While participating in the formation of an organization called La Liga Filipina, Rizal was arrested and deported to Dapitan in Zamboanga (Mindanao). During his four-year stay there, he set up a small school, opened a hospital, put up a street lighting system from money raised in a lottery, built a drainage system, introduced fishing methods, and organized a cooperative to help people deal with unscrupulous merchants. He also wrote poems and sculpted!

Andres Bonifacio and the Katipunan movement sought Rizal's support for their armed struggle, but while Rizal was sympathetic to their cause, he declined, apparently feeling that the Katipunan was not yet well enough organized and armed to have a realistic chance to win.

Rizal volunteered to work as a medic in the Spanish Cuban war and left Dapitan. While he was aboard a ship ready to sail for Cuba, the Katipunan was uncovered, the uprising was launched and many of its leaders were arrested. Rizal was implicated, was returned to Manila, tried, convicted, and shot by a firing squad on December 30, 1896, on Manila's Bagumbayan Field, the site of today's Rizal Park. He was thirty-five.

"Ultimo Adios" ("Last Farewell"), one of Rizal's best-known poems, was written the night before he was to be executed. He concealed it in the base of an alcohol lamp that he gave to his sister before going out to face the firing squad.

—The Editors

The Rizal Monument in today's Rizal Park, Manila. This is the actual spot where José Rizal was executed.

Ultimo Adiós

Adiós, Patria adorada, región del sol querida,
Perla del Mar de Oriente, nuestro perdido edén,
A darte voy, alegre, la triste mustia vida;
Y fuera más brillante, más fresca, más florida,
También por ti la diera, la diera por tu bien.

En campos de batalla, luchando con delirio,
Otros te dan sus vidas, sin dudas, sin pesar.
El sitio nada importa: ciprés, laurel o lirio,
Cadalso o campo abierto, combate o cruel martirio,
Lo mismo es si lo piden la Patria y el hogar.

Yo muero, cuando veo que el cielo se colora
Y al fin anuncia el día, tras lóbrego capuz;
Si grana necesitas, para teñir tu aurora,
¡Vierte la sangre mía, derrámala en buen hora,
Y dórela un reflejo de su naciente luz!

Mis sueños, cuando apenas muchacho adolescente,
Mis sueños cuando joven, ya lleno de vigor,
Fueron el verte un día, joya del Mar de Oriente,
Secos los negros ojos, alta la tersa frente,
Sin ceño, sin arrugas, sin manchas de rubor.

Ensueño de mi vida, mi ardiente vivo anhelo,
¡Salud! te grita el alma, que pronto va a partir;
¡Salud! ah, que es hermoso caer por darte vuelo;
Morir por darte vida, morir bajo tu cielo,
Y en tu encantada tierra la eternidad dormir!

Si sobre mi sepulcro vieres brotar, un día,
Entre la esposa yerba sencilla humilde flor,
Acércala a tus labios y besa al alma mía,
Y sienta yo en mi frente, bajo la tumba fría,
De tu ternura el soplo, de tu hálito de calor.

Deja a la luna verme, con luz tranquila y suave;
Deja que el alba envié su resplandor fugaz;
Deja gemir al viento, con su murmullo grave;
Y si desciende y posa sobre mi cruz un ave,
Deja que el ave entone su cántico de paz.

My Last Farewell

    Farewell, dear Fatherland, clime of the sun caress'd,
Pearl of the Orient seas, our Eden lost!
Gladly now I go to give thee this faded life's best,
And were it brighter, fresher, or more blest,
Still would I give it thee, nor count the cost.

    On the field of battle, 'mid the frenzy of fight,
Others have given their lives, without doubt or heed;
The place matters not—cypress or laurel or lily white,
Scaffold or open plain, combat or martyrdom's plight,
'Tis ever the same, to serve our home and country's need.

    I die just when I see the dawn break,
Through the gloom of night, to herald the day;
And if color is lacking my blood thou shalt take,
Pour'd out at need for thy dear sake,
To dye with its crimson the waking ray.

    My dreams, when life first opened to me,
My dreams, when the hopes of youth beat high,
Were to see thy lov'd face, O gem of the Orient sea,
From gloom and grief, from care and sorrow free;
No blush on thy brow, no tear in thine eye.

    Dream of my life, my living and burning desire,
All hail! Cries the soul that is now to take flight;
All hail! And sweet it is for thee to expire,
To die for thy sake, that thou mayst aspire;
And sleep in thy bosom eternity's long night.

    If over my grave some day thou seest grow,
In the grassy sod, a humble flower;
Draw it to my lips and kiss my soul so,
While I may feel on my brow in the cold tomb below
The touch of thy tenderness, my breath's warm power.

    Let the moon beam over me soft and serene,
Let the dawn shed over me its radiant flashes,
Let the wind with sad lament over me keen,
And if on my cross a bird should be seen,
Let it trill there its hymn of peace to my ashes.

Deja que el sol, ardiendo, las lluvias evapore
Y al cielo tornen puras, con mi clamor en pos;
Deja que un ser amigo mi fin temprano llore:
Y en las serenas tardes, cuando por mí alguien ore,
Ora también, oh Patria, por mi descanso a Dios.

　　Ora por todos cuantos murieron sin ventura;
Por cuantos padecieron tormentos sin igual;
Por nuestras pobres madres, que gimen su amargura;
Por huérfanos y viudas, por presos en tortura,
Y ora por ti, que veas tu redención final.

　　Y cuando, en noche oscura, se envuelva el cementerio,
Y solos sólo muertos queden velando allí.
No turbes su reposo, no turbes el misterio:
Tal vez acordes oigas de citara o salterio:
Soy yo, querida Patria, yo que te canto a ti.

　　Y cuando ya mi tumba, de todos olvidada,
No tenga cruz ni piedra que marquen su lugar,
Deja que la are el hombre, la esparza con la azada,
Y mis cenizas, antes que vuelvan a la nada,
El polvo de tu alfombra que vayan a formar.

　　Entonces nada importa me pongas en olvido:
Tu atmósfera, tu espacio, tus valles cruzaré;
Vibrante y limpia nota seré para tu oído:
Aroma, luz, colores, rumor, canto, gemido,
Constante repitiendo la esencia de mi fe.

　　Mi Patria idolatrada, dolor de mis dolores,
Querida Filipinas, oye el postrer adiós.
Ahí, te dejo todo: mis padres, mis amores.
Voy donde no hay esclavos, verdugos ni opresores;
Donde la fe no mata, donde el que reina es Dios.

　　Adiós, padres y hermanos, trozos del alma mía.
Amigos de la infancia, en el perdido hogar:
Dad gracias, que descanso del fatigoso día;
Adiós, dulce extranjera, mi amiga, mi alegria;
Adiós, queridos séres. Morir es descansar.

Let the sun draw the vapors up to the sky,
And heavenward in purity bear my tardy protest;
Let some kind soul o'er my untimely fate sigh,
And in the still evening a prayer be lifted on high
From thee, O my country, that in God I may rest.

Pray for all those that hapless have died,
For all who have suffered the unmeasur'd pain;
For our mothers that bitterly their woes have cried,
For widows and orphans, for captives by torture tried;
And then for thyself that redemption thou mayst gain.

And when the dark night wraps the graveyard around,
With only the dead in their vigil to see;
Break not my repose or the mystery profound,
And perchance thou mayst hear a sad hymn resound;
'Tis I, O my country, raising a song unto thee.

When even my grave is remembered no more,
Unmark'd by never a cross nor a stone;
Let the plow sweep through it, the spade turn it o'er,
That my ashes may carpet thy earthly floor,
Before into nothingness at last they are blown.

Then will oblivion bring to me no care,
As over thy vales and plains I sweep;
Throbbing and cleansed in thy space and air,
With color and light, with song and lament I fare,
Ever repeating the faith that I keep.

My Fatherland ador'd, that sadness to my sorrow lends,
Beloved Filipinas, hear now my last good-by!
I give thee all: parents and kindred and friends;
For I go where no slave before the oppressor bends,
Where faith can never kill, and God reigns e'er on high!

Farewell to you all, from my soul torn away,
Friends of my childhood in the home dispossessed!
Give thanks that I rest from the wearisome day:
Farewell to thee, too, sweet friend that lightened my way;
Beloved creatures all, farewell! In death there is rest!

Translation from the Spanish by Charles Derbyshire, in Hernandez, Jose Ma, et al, *A College Anthology of Rizal's Works,* Manila: R. P. Garcia Publishing Co., 1958.

Andres Bonifacio

For obvious reasons, Andres Bonifacio and the Katipunan movement are of special interest to modern nationalistic Filipinos. Though he was an admirer of Rizal, Bonifacio was different in some important ways and there are some who feel that he should be recognized as the Philippines' principal hero.

Bonifacio came from an extremely poor family and had little formal education. He founded a society with revolutionary aims; Rizal never reached the point of being a revolutionary. While Rizal was anti-friar and an activist of sorts, he was not particularly anti-Spanish. Bonifacio, on the other hand, fervently despised the Spanish. He gave up on the possibility of reform. As the founder and prime mover of the Katipunan, he may rightly be regarded as the Filipino who catalyzed the revolution of 1896.

Andres Bonifacio was born on November 30, 1863, in Tondo, Manila. His parents both died while he was very young, and young Andres helped with the support of the six children. Although he was not able to finish fourth grade, he was fond of reading and learned Spanish well, read fairly widely, and become familiar with Rizal's novels. It is said that he read books on the French Revolution of 1789 as well as on the American Revolution.

When the Manila evening newspapers of July 6, 1892 announced that José Rizal was to be banished to Dapitan on the following day, many people were infuriated. On the evening of July 7, a small group of patriotic Filipinos led by Bonifacio gathered to form what was to become the Katipunan (short for *Kataastaasan Kagalang-galang na Katipunan ng mga Anak nang Bayan,* or "Highest and Most Respectable Association of the Sons [and Daughters] of the People").

Three objectives were agreed upon: *civil*—self-help and the defense of the weak and the poor; *political*—the separation of the Philippines from Spain, or political independence; and *moral*—the teaching of good manners, hygiene and good moral character.

Attempting to organize in such a way was exceedingly dangerous, of course, so the movement was kept strictly secret. In order to minimize the danger of discovery by the Spanish authorities, a method called "triangle" was used, through which a member would recruit two new members who did not know each other. A modest initiation fee was paid by each new member. The movement's appeal was largely to urban, lower-middle and working-class Filipinos.

This proved to be a clumsy method of recruitment, and for some months the Katipunan grew very slowly. It was then agreed that all members would try to get as many new members as circumstances permitted, and this resulted in fairly rapid growth. Officers were elected and the movement experienced "growing pains" as disputes arose over leadership and anxieties about security. Working-class Filipinos found themselves impatient with the lack of fervor on the part of the leaders, who came mainly from *ilustrado* society.

Finally Bonifacio emerged and remained as the movement's main leader. A complex society developed with three kinds of membership, codes for secret communications, a flag, prescribed "commandments" (the first of which was "love God with all your heart") and teachings with a strong moral tone. The strong participation of women and teachings that showed respect and concern for women were notable for those times.

Western (and Western-trained) historians have often compared the Katipunan with such secular European revolutionary and nationalistic movements as the Levelers, Jacobins, Communists and Freemasons. But this shows a mistaken view that many Westerners have had when trying to understand Filipino peoples' movements. The Filipino historian Reynaldo Ileto points out that if we place the Katipunan in the context of Philippine history and see it in relation to other Filipino revolutionary movements, it has a distinctly religious character. Its idioms and symbols are similar to those of Christ's passion; other biblical themes are reflected in its initiation rites and other rituals. Ileto claims that this places the Katipunan squarely within the Filipino revolutionary tradition, a tradition of *pasion*.

These were tumultuous years as hysteria developed among the Spanish, who were gradually losing their grip on the situation. On August 30, 1896, martial law was declared in Manila and eight provinces of Luzon. Thousands of people were rounded up as *Katipuneros* and suspects. Many were tortured and executed. Eventually even Rizal became a victim of this hysteria, though he had disassociated himself from the movement. Finally, the secret society was betrayed. On August 19, 1896, a priest rushed to the police upon learning about it in a confessional.

This forced Bonifacio's hand. He raised his flag prematurely at Balintawak, on Manila's outskirts, and made a formal declaration of independence. On August 23, he and about five hundred companions tore up their *cedulas* (Spanish passbooks) and openly declared their willingness to fight to the death for independence. There were various skirmishes around Manila, and the fighting spread not only to other parts of Luzon, but even to the islands of Panay and Negros. Alliances had developed between the Katipunan and other movements due to the Spanish repression; some see this as the first real expression of modern Filipino nationalism. While not successful at the time, these alliances managed to transcend class and ethnic identity, an important step.

Sadly, differences between Bonifacio and Emilio Aguinaldo, a latecomer to the Katipunan and a gifted tactician and military leader, led to Bonifacio's defeat within the revolutionary movement after a period of intense infighting. This is a story in itself, involving distinct ideological positions as well as conflicting personalities. On May 10, 1897, Bonifacio was executed by a firing squad of Aguinaldo's revolutionary army.

The revolutionary movement continued, however, and while the Spanish generally contained it, their power continued to erode. There is considerable debate about what might have happened had the United States not taken power on May 1, 1898. The story of Emilio Aguinaldo's brief voluntary exile in Hong Kong, then Singapore, and his return to fight the Spanish at the request of the Americans, with the assurance that the U.S. had no interest in colonizing the Philippines, and then his betrayal by the U.S., is in itself an illuminating chapter in the history of the Filipino people.

—The Editors

References:

Agoncillo, Teodoro A. *Introduction to Filipino History,* Manila: Bookmark, 1974.

Miller, Stuart Creighton, *Benevolent Assimilation: The American Conquest of the Philippines 1899-1903,* New Haven and London: Yale U. Press, 1982. Note Miller's references to Ileto, Reynaldo Clemena, "*Pasion* and the Interpretation of Change in Tagalog Society," Ph.D. dissertation, Cornell U., 1975; and Zaide, Gregorio F., *History of the Katipunan,* Manila, 1939.

Roces, Joaquin, Ed., *Philippine Almanac Book of Facts,* 1986 Edition, Manila: Aurora Publications, 1986.

4.
IN DEFENSE OF FREEDOM

President Emilio Aguinaldo Addresses the Filipino People

Delivered at Malolos, February 5, 1899

By my proclamation of yesterday, I have published the outbreak of hostilities between the Philippine forces and the American forces of occupation in Manila, unjustly and unexpectedly provoked by the latter.

In my manifest of January 8 last I published the grievances suffered by the Philippine forces at the hands of the army of occupation. The constant outrages and taunts, which have caused the misery of the people of Manila, and, finally the useless conferences and the contempt shown the Philippine government prove the premeditated transgression of justice and liberty.

I know that war has always produced great losses; I know that the Philippine people have not yet recovered from past losses and are not in the condition to endure others. But I also know by experience how bitter is slavery, and by experience I know that we should sacrifice all on the altar of our honor and of the national integrity so unjustly attacked.

I have tried to avoid, as far as it has been possible for me to do so, armed conflict, in my endeavors to assure our independence by pacific means and to avoid more costly sacrifices. But all my efforts have been useless against the measureless pride of the American Government and of its representatives in these islands, who have treated me as a rebel because I defend the sacred interests of my country and do not make myself an instrument of their dastardly intentions.

Past campaigns will have convinced you that the people are strong when they wish to be so. Without arms we have driven from our beloved

General Emilio Aguinaldo (National Archives III-SC-98358)

country our ancient masters, and without arms we can repulse the foreign invasion as long as we wish to do so. Providence always has means in reserve and prompt help for the weak in order that they may not be annihilated by the strong; that justice may be done and humanity progress.

Be not discouraged. Our independence has been watered by the generous blood of our martyrs. Blood which may be shed in the future will strengthen it. Nature has never despised generous sacrifices.

But remember that in order that our efforts may not be wasted, that our vows may be listened to, that our ends may be gained, it is indispensable that we adjust our actions to the rules of law and of right, learning to triumph over our enemies and to conquer our own evil passions.

From Major General E. S. Otis, *Report on Military Operations and Civil Affairs in the Philippine Islands 1899*, Washington: Government Printing Office, 1899, pp. 95-96, as presented in Schirmer and Shalom, eds. *The Philippines Reader*, Boston: South End Press, 1987.

Senator Alfred J. Beveridge Addresses the U.S. Senate

Mr. President, the times call for candor. The Philippines are ours forever, "territory belonging to the United States," as the Constitution calls them. And just beyond the Philippines are China's illimitable markets. We will not retreat from either. We will not repudiate our duty in the archipelago. We will not abandon our opportunity in the Orient. We will not renounce our part in the mission of our race, trustee under God, of the civilization of the world. And we will move forward to our work, not howling out regrets like slaves whipped to their burden, but with gratitude for a task worthy of our strength, and thanksgiving to Almighty God that He has marked us as His chosen people, henceforth to lead in the regeneration of the world.

This island empire is the last land left in all the oceans. If it should prove a mistake to abandon it, the blunder once made would be irretrievable. If it proves a mistake to hold it, the error can be corrected when we will. Every other progressive nation stands ready to relieve us.

But to hold it will be no mistake. Our largest trade henceforth must be with Asia. The Pacific is our ocean. More and more Europe will manufacture the most it needs, secure from its colonies the most it consumes. Where shall we turn for consumers of our surplus? Geography answers the question. China is our natural customer. She is nearer to us than to England, Germany, or Russia, the commercial powers of the present and the future. They have moved nearer to China by securing permanent bases on her borders. The Philippines give us a base at the door of all the East.

... But if they did not command China, India, the Orient, the whole Pacific for purposes of offense, defense, and trade, the Philippines are so valuable in themselves that we should hold them. I have cruised more than 2,000 miles through the archipelago, every moment a surprise at its loveliness and wealth. I have ridden hundreds of miles on the islands, every foot of the way a revelation of vegetable and mineral riches.

No land in America surpasses in fertility the plains and valleys of Luzon. Rice and coffee, sugar and coconuts, hemp and tobacco, and many products of the temperate as well as the tropic zone grow in various sections of the archipelago.... The wood of the Philippines can supply the furniture of the world for a century to come. At Cebu the best informed man in the island told me that 40 miles of Cebu's mountain chain are practically mountains of coal....

I have a nugget of pure gold picked up in its present form on the banks of a Philippine creek. I have gold dust washed out by crude processes of careless natives from the sands of a Philippine stream. Both indicate great deposits at the source from which they come.

...It will be hard for Americans who have not studied them to understand the people. They are a barbarous race, modified by three centuries of contact with a decadent race. The Filipino is the South Sea Malay, put through a process of three hundred years of superstition in religion, dishonesty in dealing, disorder in habits of industry, and cruelty, caprice, and corruption in government. It is barely possible of self-government in the Anglo-Saxon sense.

My own belief is that there are not 100 men among them who comprehend what Anglo-Saxon self-government even means, and there are over 5,000,000 people to be governed....

Mr. President, reluctantly and only from a sense of duty am I forced to say that American opposition to the war has been the chief factor prolonging it. Had Aguinaldo not understood that in America, even in the American Congress, even here in the Senate, he and his cause were supported; had he not known that it was proclaimed on the stump and in the press of a faction in the United States that every shot his misguided followers fired into the breasts of American soldiers was like the volleys fired by Washington's men against the soldiers of King George his insurrection would have dissolved before it entirely crystallized....

But, Senators, it would be better to abandon this combined garden and Gibraltar of the Pacific, and count our blood and treasure already spent a profitable loss, than to apply any academic arrangement of self-government to these children. They are not capable of self-government. How could they be? They are not of a self-governing race. They are Orientals, Malays, instructed by Spaniards in the latter's worst estate.

... Mr. President, this question is deeper than any question of party politics; deeper than any question of the isolated policy of our country even; deeper even than any question of constitutional power. It is elemental. It is racial. God has not been preparing the English-speaking and Teutonic peoples for a thousand years for nothing but vain and idle self-contemplation and self-admiration. No! He has made us the master organizers of the world to establish system where chaos reigns. He has given us the spirit of progress to overwhelm the forces of reaction throughout the earth. He has made us adept in government that we may administer government among savage and senile peoples. Were it not for such a force as this the world would relapse into barbarism and night. And of all our race He has marked the American people as his chosen nation to finally lead in the regeneration of the world. This is the divine mission of America, and it holds for us all the profit, all the glory, all the happiness possible to man. We are trustees of all the world's progress, guardians of its righteous peace. The judgment of the Master is upon us: "Ye have been faithful over a few things; I will make you rule over many things."

Excerpts from a speech of Alfred J. Beveridge, Senator from Indiana, before the U.S. Senate. *Congressional Record,* Senate, Jan. 9, 1900, pp. 704-711. (Note the section "The Americans Arrive" in Mananzan's chapter in *Rice in the Storm.)*

Other Voices

General Arthur MacArthur (National Archives 165-PF-2)

When I first started in against these rebels I believed that Aguinaldo's troops represented only a fraction.... I did not like to believe that the whole population of Luzon...was opposed to us, but having come thus far, and having been brought much in contact with both insurgents and amigos, I have been reluctantly compelled to believe that the Filipinos masses are loyal to Aguinaldo and the government which he leads.

_{Statement of General Arthur MacArthur to an American war correspondent, published in the *New York Criterion* of June 17, 1899, subsequently corroborated by MacArthur in his testimony before the Senate in 1902 (Senate Doc. 331, pt. 2, 57th Congress., 1st Session, p. 1942).}

* * *

Taking into account the disadvantages they have to fight against in arms, equipment and military discipline, without artillery, short of ammunition, powder inferior, shells reloaded until they are defective, inferior in every particular of equipment and supplies, they are the bravest men I have ever seen.... What we want is to stop this accursed war.... These men are indomitable. At Bacoor bridge they waited until the Americans had brought their cannon to within thirty-five yards of their trenches. Such men have the right to be heard. All they want is a little justice.

Statement of General Henry W. Lawton, C.E. Russell, *The Outlook for the Philippines,* as cited by Storey and Lichauco in *The Conquest of the Philippines,* New York: Putnam's Sons, 1926.

* * *

...This war, if you call it war, has gone on for three years. It will go on in some form for three hundred years, unless this policy is abandoned. You will undoubtedly have times of peace and quiet, or pretended submission. You will buy men with titles or officers or salaries. You will intimidate cowards. You will get pretended and fawning submission. The land will smile and smile and seem at peace. But the volcano will be there. The lava will break out again. You can never settle this thing until you settle it right.

From a speech in the U.S. Senate by Senator George F. Hoar, May 22, 1902.

New York World, 1898

All, of Whatever Race or Color, Are Entitled to Life, Liberty and the Pursuit of Happiness

We earnestly condemn the policy of the present National Administration in the Philippines. It seeks to extinguish the spirit of 1776 in those islands. We deplore the sacrifice of our soldiers and sailors, whose bravery deserves admiration even in an unjust war. We denounce the slaughter of the Filipinos as a needless horror. We protest against the extension of American sovereignty by Spanish methods.

We demand the immediate cessation of the war against liberty, begun by Spain and continued by us. We urge that Congress by promptly convened to announce to the Filipinos our purpose to concede to them the independence for which they have so long fought and which of right is theirs.

... We hold, with Abraham Lincoln, that "no man is good enough to govern another without that man's consent. When the white man governs himself, that is self-government, but when he governs himself and also governs another man, that is more than self-government—this is despotism."

We cordially invite the cooperation of all men and women who remain loyal to the Declaration of Independence and the Constitution of the United States.

Excerpts from the platform of the American Anti-Imperialist League, 1899. From *Speeches, Correspondence and Political Papers of Carl Schurz*, ed. Frederic Bancroft. New York: G.P. Putnam's Sons, 1913, Vol. VI. As presented in *The Philippines Reader*, ed. Schirmer and Shalom, Boston: South End Press, 1987.

We Are a World Power
by Mark Twain

We are a world power, no one can deny it, a brass-gilt one, a tuppence, ha'penny one, but a World Power just the same. We have bought some islands from a party that did not own them; with real smartness and a good counterfeit of disinterested friendliness, we coaxed a weak nation into a trap, and closed it upon them; we went back on our honored guest of the stars and stripes when we had no further use for him, and chased him into the mountains; we are as indisputably in possession of a wide-spreading archipelago as if it were our own property; we have pacified some thousands of islanders and buried them; destroyed their fields; burned their villages and turned their widows and orphans out of doors; furnished their heart-breaking exile to dozens of disagreeable patriots and subjugated the remaining millions by Benevolent Assimilation which is the pious new name of the musket; we have acquired property in the three hundred concubines and other slaves of our business partner, the Sultan of Sulu, and hoisted our protecting flag over that swag.

And so, by these providences of God—the phrase is the Government's, not mine—we are a World Power; and are glad, and proud, and have a Back Seat in the Family. With tacks in it. At least we are letting on to be glad and proud; and it is the best way. Indeed, it is the only way. We must maintain our dignity, for the people are looking. We are a World Power, we cannot get out of it now, and we must make the best of it.

From *Mark Twain in Eruption,* ed. Bernard De Voto, New York: Grosset & Dunlap, 1940.

Letters from the Philippines

The following are excerpts from letters and diaries of United States servicemen who were sent to fight in the Philippine-American War. This was the longest voyage American troops had ever undertaken for war, and some realized at the time that it was the beginning of a new epoch in history.

It was a violent period and a terrible war. Accounts vary as to how many persons died, with estimates starting at 200 thousand Filipino lives lost as a direct result of the war. General Bell estimated that one-sixth of the population of Luzon had died, which would bring the total to an astounding 600 thousand deaths.

The collection of documents, diaries, letters, interviews, official military accounts, newspaper articles and cartoons from that era reflect both brutality and tenderness, both openmindedness and vicious racism, both homesickness and affection for a beautiful and interesting land. Here are some of the more humanizing items.

* * *

"May 25, 1898—set sail for the Philippines. Crossed the bar at 5:45 p.m., enthusiastic, sick...."

"... Advised by the doctor to take a walk, so accompanied by sergeants Grimm and Callister, I did. We were all over the native city of Cavite, it was quite a sight. Houses are built of bamboo, about 4 feet off the ground, and roofed with leaves. We could see no gardens to speak of, nor land in cultivation. They seem to live on fruit gathered from outside, and fish. In some places they would give us fruit...."

"... The town is all covered with shade trees of all descriptions. The streets are narrow, and dirty, the sidewalks about two feet wide. Many two wheeled carts and small ponies. The natives would give anything for a pistol, or watch. The natives are very polite and pleasant. They look like the Japs. They think we're the gods of war, we're so large compared to them. It's very amusing to see them watch us. I talked Spanish as far as I could with some of them, and find them somewhat educated. The women during trading raise the prices manyfold. Money is scarce with us—the boys trade knives, razors, safety pins, hardtack, anything. The natives are shrewd, and don't get fooled...."

"... There are three Spanish cathedrals in the town. One of them has the date 1642 on it. From what I can find out, though, the others are still older than this one. Went through one of them, but I took a great risk in doing so, as the natives are ardent Catholics, and don't want to allow anyone into one of these churches just for sightseeing. I went in at the door, but was met by a native priest who was not going to allow me to enter. But I talked to him awhile. Of course he couldn't understand a word I said, and finally he led the way inside. He knelt and crossed himself, and looked rather doubtful at me when I made no demonstration but to take off my hat. The altar images were beautiful. Tapers burning at a shrine which was draped with blue silk. Some of the images were wax. The inside of the church was frescoed in artistic style, but rather dim with age. In a big notch in the floor was a big pipe organ. The ivory keys were yellow with age. In the stone floor were set marble plaques with dates and inscriptions of those lying beneath. After about 5 minutes the priest grew impatient, so I went out...."

"Until the last days I never thought that there would be any fighting between us and the natives. But things now look very serious. We may avoid a scrap, but if so it would be an accident. For if we should pursue our present policy of annexing the islands, the Filipinos are going to fight, and I don't see how we can retreat from the stand which we have taken. General Otis' proclamation was hardly published before the open, defiant rejoinder of Aguinaldo was posted on all the walls of this city. It is the general opinion that Aguinaldo has matched Otis himself in generalship and diplomacy. Otis' proclamation is a masterpiece, and so is Aguinaldo's answer. There is no denying the fact that while we have been led to believe that the Filipinos were fighting among themselves, and were ready to send their leader out of camp in disgrace, instead, Aguinaldo has gathered around him strong men of his people, strengthening his outposts around Manila, arming the army, filling his treasure with wealth of money and kind, bringing back the faltering, encouraging the faithful. Thus when our bugle blasts are sounded, instead of seeing all roads blocked with the surging mass of Filipinos on the way to the marketplace, we get for an answer, 'give us our independence, or we fight you to the death.' We are told that history repeats itself. Aguinaldo has become a George Washington, and Otis a Sir Henry Gill; Manila, New York; Malolos, Philadelphia.''

"... Guadalupe where we are is a beautiful native village of considerable size on the bank of the Pasig. Small hills surround us on every side. The valleys are filled with rice fields and banana groves now lying desolate. I believe that a more beautiful country never existed. Why these native people have chosen to fight their benefactors rather than to remain at peace and grow wealthy from their rich land is more than I can understand...."

"... Pasig was a beautiful city. It's situated on an island in the river. But in a few hours it will be in ashes. This house where I now abide is a marvel of native ingenuity. And only a few days ago it was the home of a family, and perhaps a happy one. Its well-thatched roof and clean rooms, a well-kept garden, and fish traps, indicates to me a thrifty family. But where are its people? Perhaps the mother and children are wandering around, while the father has fallen before the many who wish to kill, or maybe they lie encamped behind a trench which will soon be the scene of agony and death...."

From the soundtrack of *First in the Philippines,* a video about the Oregon Volunteers, a National Guard unit that set sail for the Philippines on May 25, 1898, and stayed there for about two years. Produced by Robert Koglin, Center for the Moving Image, Portland State University, Portland, Oregon, 1984.

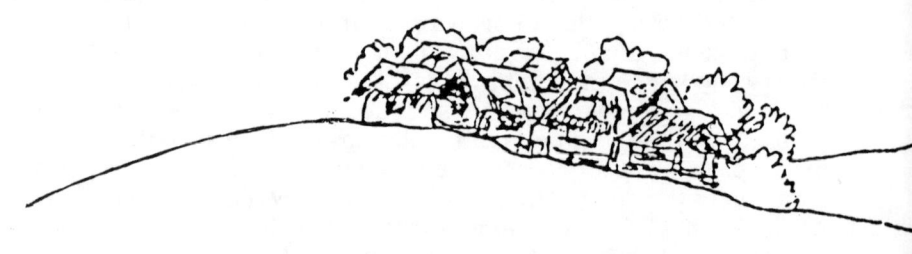

5. TOWARD A SOVEREIGN NATION

The Philippine National Anthem

The Philippine National Anthem was first played on June 12, 1898, by the musical band of San Francisco de Malabon on the occasion of the proclamation of Philippine independence. It was composed by Julian Felipe, a music teacher and composer, with words written by Jose Palma, a poet and soldier. It was at the suggestion of General Mariano Trias that Felipe went to President Aguinaldo's residence and played a rough draft of the march was presented to Aguinaldo, Trias and other leaders of the revolution, who agreed to officially adopt it as the "Marcha Nacional Filipina." Palma's original Spanish lyrics were given Tagalog and English translations in the 1920s. Today, guidelines for the proper use of the anthem state that it should always be sung in Pilipino (the national language, based on Tagalog), whether in the Philippines or abroad.

Pambansang Awit

Philippine National Anthem

*Spanish original by Jose Palmo

J. Felipe
Ed. Janice Johnson

*English Translation by Camilo Osias and M.A.L. Lane. Tagalog Version, Department Order No. 5, Series 1956

The Philippine Flag

When the Spanish arrived in the Philippines there was nothing that could be called a national flag, though there were banners representing regions or clans. During the Spanish period it was considered treason to fly any flag except the Spanish flag.

The Philippine flag evolved during the last years of Spanish rule. Its first stage was that of the flag of the Katipunan, which was raised at the Cry of Balintawak in 1896. This flag displayed the sun that is seen on the modern Philippine flag. Its second stage was that of Bonifacio's war standard used in the Cavite campaign against the Spaniards. This flag featured a more prominent, stylized sun. The third flag was designed by General Emilio Aguinaldo and his followers while they were in Hong Kong. It was raised during the proclamation of Philippine independence in Cavite.

When the Americans completed their conquest of the Philippines, they forbade the use of any flag except the American flag, fearing that flying the Philippine flag might unduly awaken Philippine nationalism. It was therefore a crime for Filipinos to fly their own flag in their own country! In 1919, however, Governor General Francis B. Harrison authorized the flying of the Philippine flag alongside the American flag.

In 1936, at the beginning of Commonwealth Government, President Manuel L. Quezon decreed the fourth and present flag, patterned after that of General Aguinaldo, to be the country's official flag.

From "The Flag of our Fathers," by Domingo Abella, as presented in *The Philippine Almanac*, 1986 Edition. Manila: Aurora Publications, pp. 281-282.

On the Philippine flag, the sun represents liberty, its eight rays stand for the eight provinces that rose up in rebellion in 1896, and the three stars are for the geographic divisions of Luzon, the Visayas and Mindanao.

6.
IMAGES FROM PROTESTANT MISSION

Staunton of Sagada

"I beg to introduce to you the Rev. J.A. Staunton, Jr." So stated the Rt. Rev. Charles Henry Brent, Bishop of the Philippines, in a pamphlet printed in Boston in the summer of 1916.

"He is a man of extraordinary gifts; he has been in the highest of all universities since he went out to the Philippine Islands—the university of hardship, both of body and of mind. He has been misunderstood—at times even by myself. It is only comparatively recently that I have given the man his full measure. The mission that he represents is not a station, it is a diocese. He is the chief spiritual influence of that entire country. His advice is sought by the officials who represent the American Government there; he is working on friendly terms with the Roman Catholic clergy who are laboring in that district... [If] there were times when I thought that I could teach Fr. Staunton better ways of doing his work than those he had learned from God himself, I have ceased to inject my own theories into the life of a man who has proved by his work that he knows how to bring simple-minded people into close and intimate touch with God as revealed in Jesus Christ...."

* * *

In June of 1904 Father Staunton accompanied Father Clapp up to Bontoc, sleeping in the old Spanish *camarin* in Sagada en route, and there he spent the worst months of the rainy season getting ready for the move to his new station... and on October 2nd Father Staunton baptized his first native Sagadan.

Mrs. Staunton arrived in December and began what was to be a long and loving career of ministering to the Igorots' sick bodies and need for sympathy. The old men of Sagada were meanwhile approached for their approval to establish a mission in the town itself, and a large area was assigned for this use in consideration of the facts that modern education would be good for their grandchildren and wage-earning employment good for their sons. . . .

Here the Stauntons moved into an abandoned goat shed twelve feet square in April 1905, where for three months they lived, taught school, conducted a dispensary, celebrated divine services and baptized more than a hundred converts, while the engineer-priest laid his plans for a little Christian metropolis in the midst of a pagan wilderness. . . .

Mrs. Staunton gave out medicine and went around the town making house calls, and quickly set a pattern of compassion that has become legendary by venturing out at night in tropical storms on horseback. A large woman handicapped by the garments and undergarments of her day, she would crawl through the waist-high doorways of Igorot houses to make her visitations; she learned to speak Igorot and was known to make calls in which she could name all the children and inquire intelligently about relatives and in-laws. Father Staunton, meanwhile, conducted two services daily, gave instruction in hymn-singing and devotional exercises to almost 40 Christians and pagans, and made trips to neighboring villages to invite people to Christian worship in the municipal center.

Attendance at Sunday services averaged 70, including those who had hiked in from Bagnen, Ankileng, Nacagan, Balugan, Alab, Tetepan, Tanulong, Fidelesan, Agawa and Besao. In June Bishop Brent made his first visitation, consecrated the cemetery where four Christians had already been laid to rest, and confirmed 50 souls in Bagnen and 63 in Sagada. Having established his ministry, Father Staunton turned his attention toward creating that plant which was later to be called "an engineer's dream."

Sagada's pioneer missionary was unable to find skilled or dependable labor locally so he hired American, Chinese and Japanese workmen from Manila, and appointed Senor Masferre overall supervisor. A Mr. S.J. Douglas came up after building Easter School in Baguio to install a sawmill at the foot of a waterfall in pineclad Fidelesan, four miles away, which was in operation in 1907, selling lumber to the Government in Bontoc in 1908, and was self-supporting and employing 40 natives by 1912. Mrs. Staunton's medical ministry was greatly extended by the arrival of Dr. Radcliffe Johnson and his family in April, 1907, and that same year Father Staunton was operating, in addition to the sawmill itself, a planer, a shingle-mill, lime-kiln and charcoal pits, had opened a stone quarry, constructed a very respectable church, and was directing such diverse activities as logging, carpentering, blacksmithing, repair work, blasting, excavation and stonecutting. . . .

When the Stauntons finally moved into a permanent American-style house in 1912, the policy of importing lowland workers to train the local people had borne fruit: 14 native stone masons were employed under a Japanese foreman, an Igorot boy was skillfully occupied in full-time manufacture and care of stone chisels, and a Chandler & Price job press was being operated by one of the boys the Stauntons had taken into their home. And this was only the beginning.

The next year Father Staunton's enterprises had become so vast that the annual report of the Mission of St. Mary the Virgin covered 21 printed pages in the Convocation Journal and was written by eight different people.

By 1915, just ten years after he first settled in Sagada, the Mission was already known as one of the outstanding achievements of the American occupation of the Philippine Islands. Visitors intrepid enough to reach the savage heights of the Cordillera Central on horseback could stand on the Staunton's stone verandah and look down in dumbfounded amazement at 80 acres of activities connected by 20 miles of telephone wire. Four stone quarries were in operation and two lime kilns; long lines of Igorots carried lumber in from the Fidelesan sawmill and a planing mill reduced it to timber, boards and shingles; electric-lighted gasoline-powered machine and carpenter shops turned out tools and furnishings. Sweet spring water was piped into the compound under sufficient pressure to make coiled firehoses practical in many of the 20 buildings which housed the shops, stores, supplies and considerable herd of cows, water-buffalo and horses. Vegetables were grown both by schoolboys and professional gardeners; the Mission employed a shoemaker, tailor and laundress; and schoolgirls were already producing salable lace and handwoven cloth. Photographs of the day (developed and printed locally) show American lady missionaries with pompadours pouring tea at wicker tables in rose-trellised gardens, and Father Staunton himself dictated letters to a secretary on stationery printed on his own press in an office with three telephones on his desk. Fifty apprentices were under industrial training and 150 others on the payroll, 175 school children under instruction, and the beautiful frame church where daily services were conducted listed 2,000 baptisms and 600 communicants, all of whom were privileged to make purchases in the Igorot exchange whose $10,000 worth of stock had been hauled in on bullcarts over a trail surveyed by the Priest-in-Charge himself.

It was the opinion of those older Sagadans interviewed when collecting data for the present article that Father Staunton loved them as he loved himself because he wanted them to have good things. This is no small reputation. . . .

Ironically, Sagada's own progress had made Father Staunton's position untenable without increased funds. That magnificent edifice whose construction had provided steady employment for a decade was consecrated on December 8, 1921, and a small army of laborers, stonemasons, carpenters, machine-operators, mechanics, carters and printers could find no new employer for their skills. Projects then under development like the combined hospital and high school, which was to function as neither, would aggravate rather than relieve the financial pressure. . . . Worst of all was the lurking fear that the Christian way of life had not yet been firmly enough fixed to ensure continued adherence by the newly unemployed.

* * *

. . . . The man of whom Bishop Brent was speaking was a missionary as great and as well known as Brent himself, the founder and Priest-in-Charge of the Mission of St. Mary the Virgin in Sagada, a station remarkable alike for its originality, grand vision and execution; and the aggressive devotion with which it was hewn into being. Ten years later this same man was to be back in America looking for a job and fifteen years later was to reject his priestly vows and request deposition that he might make his submission to the Church of Rome. Such was the truly meteoric career of Staunton of Sagada, Christian Civilizer.

Excerpts from "Staunton of Sagada: Christian Civilizer," by William Henry Scott, in *The Historical Magazine* of the Protestant Episcopal Church, Vol. XXXI, No. 4, December 1962.

Selections from Missionary Letters

"Are you afraid of tiki—little house lizards? There are many who live inside my house as well as on the outside. I talk to them sometimes and call them Beady-Eyes. I used to think that their main diet was insects, but I find they look for crumbs on my table or beside the sink. One time when I baked brownies, I put them on my bed to cool. Before they completely cooled, I found a tiki crawling on top of them. It is fun to watch the tiki on the outside of my window screens at night. Apparently the females always have twins as two eggs are plainly seen through their transparent stomachs. And if a tiki loses its tail in a fight, it gradually grows a new tail. The people say these lizards are very religious because at 6:00 p.m. they go down on the ground to pray. I'm not so sure about that."

Charlotte Houck
Wycliff Bible Translators
September 1985

Caroling: Christmas Serenade. Accompanied by guitar and other improvised "musical instruments" such as soft drink bottle caps strung into bells, people of all ages go caroling during the Christmas season. Pen and ink by Orlando Castillo, 1986.

"Noel's responsibilities for Bible translation projects now involve computerization, or word processing, for four translation teams. This new technological wonder makes it possible for each team to have its own portable computer, so that the text is keyed in only once. All successive revisions and corrections in the translation process can be made on the computer without the need for retyping the whole Bible six times, as in the past.

Most of the translation projects he supervises are interconfessional, that is, Protestant and Catholic translators and reviewers do the work. He travels to four sites in the Philippines to do checking. A revision of the 1980 Tagalog [national language] Bible is now underway in Manila.... This December the Samarenyo [language of Eastern Visayan Islands] Bible will be published and dedicated. The Ibanag [language group of northeast Luzon] New Testament should be finished in 1985. The Bikol Bible for southeastern Luzon will be completed in 1986.... In 1987, the Pampango [central Luzon] Bible is expected to be finalized. These are the major translation projects now of the Philippine Bible Society."

> Noel and Emma Ruth Osborn
> United Methodist missionaries
> United Bible Society
> October 1984

"This has been a year of disasters. A typhoon brought terrible floods in May. I could not reach the session of my annual conference due to impassable roads. You probably heard about the earthquake and tidal waves which struck Mindanao two weeks ago today. The tremor was not felt in Manila and the damage was centered around the Moro Gulf about 600 miles to the south. The latest government report is 4,800 dead, 2,800 missing, and 50,000 houses and 4,000 fishing boats washed away. The tidal waves caused the greater damage and the fishermen who live along the coast suffered most...."

> Byron W. Clark
> United Methodist missionary
> 1976

"I am in Manila again with stacks of paperwork to do but I have been able to spend quite a bit of time these last few weeks in the mountains where I belong but my heart is so overflowing this morning that I want to share it with you....

The Quirino area is an extensive mountainous area northeast of Imugan. The slopes are more gentle there than around Imugan but there are fewer roads. The area was only recently opened by loggers but now people, many of them Christians from other mountain churches, are moving in.

Pastor Danny Bugtong, Pastor Lazaro Dallego, Ramon Oliano and I hiked in with Romy Paay, a new graduate of our Bible School. Danny preached an evangelistic message in each community in the evenings and I conducted free-wheeling discussions in the mornings. Our discussions ranged all over the field including health, medicinal plants, the interpretation of some difficult passages in Revelation and in Luke, land rights, environmental protection, and how to plant fruit trees. We swam one river and hiked more than 50 kilometers to visit these new outreaches but it was a wonderful experience and well worth the effort....

One of our most difficult programs is the financial assistance we give to some pastors who are directly involved in outreach. I say "difficult" because it could make a congregation dependent and damage its sense of responsibility. Our leaders are handling it very well, however, and two of the congregations asked to be removed from the list of subsidized congregations last week. They are not yet strong congregations but they are determined to be on their own without "nursing" from the Parish Funds. The funds thus released are now available for other outreaches. There are so many answers to prayers recently that it is hard to keep up with them."

Delbert Rice
United Methodist missionary
Kalahan Cooperative Parish
May 1987

Pasko sa Kanayunan: Christmas in the Barrio. Christmas in the barrio evokes the celebration of its resources: the land, nature's bounty, and its most important resource, the Filipino peasants. Pen and ink by Orlando Castillo, 1986.

7. THE STRUGGLE CONTINUES

Father Rosaleo ("Rudy") Romano, a Redemptorist priest in Cebu City, was abducted on July 11, 1985, by armed men later identified as government military intelligence agents. Fr. Romano, who was known for his courageous human rights advocacy, was never seen again. Desmond Egan, who wrote this tribute, is a poet from Ireland working in the Philippines.

For Father Romano on His 45th Birthday
by Desmond Egan

in you Romano I salute the few
who hand out like bread to others
their ordinary life
and build up block by block
anonymous in the loneliest villages
their chapel to the spirit

who bear witness in remote marketplaces
wearing white against the sun
who make their flesh and blood an angelus
pealing across huts and plots
deeper than bullhorn or gunfire
than any saluting officers who imagine they
can bundle truth into a jeep
and stub out freedom with cigarette butts
and build walls higher than the sky
and riddle with foreign rifles
the soul they think they have blindfolded

in you Romano I salute every
missionary of hope
especially if I may the unsung Irish
the ones who have scattered themselves like seed
across all forgotten worlds

and when I hear that such as they as you
have ended up in prisons or ditches
I feel as well as rage a fierce pride a
joy of sorts at this reminder
that the resurrection continues

Romano your persecutors will only succeed
in squeezing from your body the blood of Christ
and though they dump you in one compound or another
your soul flies with ease up over
their pathetic cement their money sentries
their rusting barbed wire
flies across the globe makes people like us your family
who would otherwise never have known you
and in your name we join hands
fall into step and sing together
the song of your life
no one can stop our march

Ed de la Torre

happy are those who dream dreams and are willing to pay the price to make their dreams come true

An Agape Celebration

using plain cooked rice and water

Celebrant 1: An agape meal is a celebration of our brotherhood and sisterhood, our unity. The Jewish passover meal celebrates the liberation from Egypt. The Eucharist was instituted during that meal in memory of Christ's life and to celebrate the power of life over death.

Celebrant 2: By sharing a meal in common we are united in a sacred pact. We share equally the food and drink that is available. It is God's will to give the gifts of creation, the goods of the earth, to all people, so that they might build a more humane world.

Celebrant 3: In the agape meal (tonight) we have rice to share. Human hands and bare feet plowed the fields. Thorns cut the farmer's feet. At home at night, the farmer chills. Seedlings are planted. When the field needs watering the farmer keeps watch all night walking back and forth from the source of water to the fields. Harrowing is done with ox-like *carabaos* that pull the iron "combs." Bodies bend and pull to weed the fields. They cut the palay or grain and gather it into sheaves. Threshing is done with their feet. Winnowing, they whistle, calling the wind to drive away the chaff. Three cans of palay* are put into one bag, which the farmer carries on his back. The rice mill is hot, dark and dusty. Workers make ten dollars a month.

All: Blessed are you, God of all creation. Through your goodness we have rice to share. Let it become for us the food of liberation.

* *unhusked rice.*

Celebrants serve plain, cooked rice to the congregation in small bowls. Each worshipper is invited to take a "pinch" of rice.

Celebrant 1: In the agape meal (tonight) we have water to share. The people in upland Cavite get their water by climbing down one hundred and fifty steep steps to the spring. They use pails that are drawn together by a stick over their shoulders. Children eight, nine years old carry heavy pails. In many homes there is only one glass, one communal drinking glass.

Celebrant 2: The people in Campo Uno Bukidnon depend on rain water. In the summers the roads are dusty, and the dust settles on the roof. The rain water collected often makes the people sick.

Celebrant 3: The Samaritan woman offered a drink of water to Jesus. Jesus' promise of living water is Good News!

All: Blessed are you, God of all creation. Through your goodness we have water to share. Let it become for us the living water of justice and righteousness.

Celebrants serve the worshippers a small drink of water.

Celebrant 1: Nourish us with your love, good and gracious God, that we may embrace life with the full power given to us. Open our hearts to Christ, who comes not to take away our struggle but to be with us in it. Guide us in our work and worship together that we may act to bring about the reign of God on earth.

From the *Guide to Worship,* National Ecumenical Conference on the Philippines, Berkeley, California, Nov. 13-15, 1987.

UNICEF/Jim Wright

Who Am I?
by Elizabeth Tapia

I am woman
  I am Filipino
    I am alive
      I am struggling
        I am hoping.

    I am created in the image of God
      just like all other people in the world;
    I am a person with worth and dignity.
    I am a thinking person, a feeling person,
    a doing person.
    I am the small *I am* that stands before the
    big *I AM*.

    I am a witness to the moans, tears, banners and
      clenched fists of my people.
    I can hear their liberating songs, their hopeful
      prayers and decisive march toward justice
      and freedom.

    I believe that all of us—women and men
      young and old, Christian and non-Christian
      are called upon to do responsible action;
        to be concerned
        to be involved

      NOW.

I am hoping
  I am struggling
  I am alive
  I am Filipino
    I am a woman.

Elizabeth Tapia, a United Methodist minister, was consultant on women's concerns for the Christian Conference of Asia. From *No Longer Strangers,* World Council of Churches, 1984.

P.B. – Pastor ng Bayan   "EXODUS"

This is just like Exodus. God told Moses that he will take his people from the land of bondage into the promised land.

God defeated the oppressive Pharaoh of Egypt and freed his chosen people.

Because of this, the Israelites believed in God and in Moses.

We also believe, Pastor. But what about us? From "no man's land," we are going to the land of bondage? Where is the promised land?

Is this the promised land? Where is Junior? There is no place to sleep? Pastor, where do we get food? What about our carabaos and farm? We need medicine, Baby has LBM.

'Okay, we have now decided on a course of action...'

'Thus says Yahweh: Let my people go!'

"P.B." stands for "Pastor ng Bayan," or Pastor of the People. From *Simbayan*, Ecumenical Center for Development, April 1984 and August 1984.

The Immortal Words of Macli-ing

Macli-ing Dulag, a leader of the Kalinga people of the mountains of Northern Luzon, stood courageously against the building of the Chico Dam project, which would have resulted in the flooding of the Kalinga ancestral lands. He was killed in his home on the night of April 24, 1980 by a unit of the Armed Forces of the Philippines. In reading this we cannot help but think of the sad and poetic lament of the Native American leader, Chief Seattle.

What is the most precious thing to human beings? Life! If life is threatened, what ought persons do? Resist. This they must do, otherwise they are dishonored and that is a worse death. If we do not fight and the dams push through, we die anyway. If we fight, we die honorably. I exhort you all, then—fight!

Because we are willing to fight now our children may win and keep this Kalinga land. And the land shall become even more sacred when nourished by our sweat and blood. Then we who sacrificed that they might live and be secure and happy shall stay with them and nurture the generations, guarding the fields and the villages, blessing their lives 'til endless time.

To a government official: You ask if we own the land and mock us, saying, "Where is your title?" When we ask the meaning of your words you answer with taunting arrogance, "Where are the documents to prove that you own the land?" Such arrogance to speak of owning the land when we instead are owned by it. How can you own that which will outlive you? Only the race owns the land, because the race lives forever. To claim a place is the birthright of every person. The lowly animals claim their place—how much more human beings!

Humanity is born and lives. Apu Kabuni-an, Lord of us all, gave us life and placed us in the world to live human lives. And where shall we obtain life? From the land! To work the land is an obligation, not merely a right. In tilling the land you possess it. And so land is a grace that must be nurtured. To enrich it and make it fructify is the eternal exhortation of Apu Kabuni-an to all his children. Land is sacred, and is beloved. From its womb springs our Kalinga life.

8.
A RICH AND GRACEFUL CULTURE

From the Writings of Carlos Bulosan

. . . I knew that if there was one redeeming quality in our poverty, it was this boundless affinity for each other, this humanity that grew in each of us, as boundless as this green earth.

Luciano, who was next to my brother Leon, was in Camp Stotsenburg* completing his three-year service in the Philippine Scouts, a native detachment of the United States Army. Macario, who was next to him, was a student at the high school in Lingayen, the capital of the province of Pangasinan. It was for Macario that we were all working so hard, so that he could come back to Binalonan to teach school and, perhaps, to help us support our large family. . . .

But now it was Amado's job, when plowing time came, to follow my father with a bamboo harrow until the land was cleared, leveled, and ready for planting. I did the cooking and other simple chores in the house. The work on the farm was heavy and every hand was needed until the harvest was over. But there were gratifying compensations in the depth of my childhood.

At sundown my father told me to take our animals into the corral. It was a clear evening and he wanted to work with my brother into the night. I pulled our *carabaos* and goats from their pegs in the pasture and drove them to our house. I hitched a little bamboo sled to the largest goat and went to the village well with three empty petroleum cans. Many people were waiting to fill their earthen drinking jars or to water their working animals. When my turn came, I lowered the wooden bucket into the deep well and tied the end of the rope to a papaya tree; then I pulled it up slowly and laboriously to the mouth of the well and poured the water carefully into the cans. Before the cans were full many people had arrived and were waiting for their turn.

* Now called Clark Air Base.

B. David Williams

I walked ahead of the docile goat, and it followed me obediently to our house. I filled the water trough in the corral and the animals stopped chewing the dry rice stalks. They came anxiously to the trough and plunged their muzzles into the water, their throats making gulping noises as the cold water thundered into their stomachs. I carried the remaining can of water into the house and filled the earthen drinking jars on the makeshift stand by the wall.

The night came at last and darkness filled the house; except for the tiny needles of light that filtered through the walls from the sky, there was no other illumination. I found the small oil lamp where my father kept it in the bamboo rack under the homemade pillows. I lighted it and went to the kitchen. There was no food left. I went to the rice bin and filled the cooking pot. I prepared string beans and mixed them with small slices of beef. When the pot began to bubble on the roaring stove, I heard my father and brother coming noisily through the gate with their implements. They went to the water trough to wash their feet and hands; then they came into the house and asked me if dinner was ready.

We sat on the floor and ate in the twilight with our bare hands. We spread the salted fish on the steaming rice and soaked it with the broth from the vegetable pot. When we finished eating my father started washing the polished coconut shells which had been our plates and drinking cups for many generations. I went outside the house to feed our dog with cold rice. Amado followed and watched me, out of habit. Then my father came out also and sat on a long log under the eaves, and we talked about our farm for hours, centering our thoughts around my brother Macario, who was our pride and the star of all our hope. When midnight came we went to bed because we would have to be up early in the morning.

From Carlos Bulosan. *America is in the Heart,* Seattle and London: University of Washington Press, 1973. First printed by Harcourt, Brace and Co., Inc., in 1943.

Postnatal Care

By Juan M. Flavier, M.D.

I stopped by the fence as courtesy demanded. We had just come from the toilet-bowl-making demonstration so my pants were splattered with cement.

"*Nagtanim ka yata ng palay sa bukid ah* (You seem to have planted rice in the field)!" Mang Teroy greeted me.

"*Hindi, nagtanim ng semento* (No, I planted cement)," I answered. "You seem to be dressed to kill. Where are you going?"

Mang Teroy came near me and said, "I am going to Martin's place, my nephew. I heard he just slaughtered a chicken."

"What does it mean? Is there a special occasion?" I inquired.

He came ever nearer and whispered to me, "Yes, either the chicken is sick or someone is sick in the household."

I could not help smiling.

Martin was about nineteen years old and had been married for about a year and a half. He had some business inclination. In the course of buying and selling clothes and slippers from town to town, he had met Lita. After they got married, Martin convinced Lita to settle temporarily with his parents in the barrio.

Mang Teroy knew that Martin was like a member of my family. When Martin was about fourteen years old, he had taken care of my youngest son. He had babysat for us and tended our pets, including a duck, a goat, and a turkey.

Since I had not seen Martin and his wife for quite some time, I joined Mang Teroy. Or maybe I wanted to find out whether the chicken was sick or someone was sick in his household.

The nipa hut was beside the elementary school and directly along the main road.

As we entered the yard, we could not help noticing the two *tiklis* (big wide-mouthed baskets) filled with native chickens.

"It looks as though there will be a fiesta here," Mang Teroy commented.

"No, *Tiyong* (uncle)," Martin answered with a wide smile. "But with Doctor Flavier visiting me—that calls for a feast."

I patted his back affectionately. "How is Lita?" I inquired.

"She is well and is upstairs," Martin answered. "She is due to have our first baby next month, that is why her mother arrived bringing this tiklis of chickens."

"That is too much *pasalubong* (homecoming gift)," Mang Teroy commented.

"What can you do if Martin is her favorite son-in-law?" I said, winking at Martin. I knew he was the only son-in-law.

We sat on a bench which someone brought down to the yard. "Let us sit here as it is too hot inside the house," Martin said.

"So you have chicken every day?" Mang Teroy asked.

"No, Tiyong, those chickens are for Lita's postpartum (*pagka-anak*)," Martin answered. He looked toward the window of the house to see if his mother-in-law was in hearing distance. In a lower voice he continued, "Where my mother-in-law comes from, a wife who has just delivered a baby must be fed with chicken every day for thirty days to make her recover her strength fast. Also, the chicken is stewed with malunggay (Moringa Olcifera) leaves to induce her milk for the baby's sustenance. And the chicken must be the native kind."

"The rest makes sense," I whispered back, "but why native chickens? I would think a white leghorn is just as good."

"I do not know, doctor, but my mother-in-law said a white leghorn chicken is *malansa* (fishy), which is bad for a postpartum (bagong anak)," Martin explained.

I looked at the chicken in the tiklis. "Anyway, she brought native chickens so you have no cause to complain."

"Is there a medical basis?" Martin wanted to know.

"For fishy chicken being bad for postpartum mothers?" I tried to think of a possible scientific explanation. "Not that I know of."

Mang Teroy came nearer to listen to the conversation being carried on in a low tone. "How about the daily chicken menu and the malunggay?" he asked.

"Of course, those are good for the mother and the baby," I answered still in a soft voice. "Chicken is good protein and malunggay is one of our highest and most available iron-containing vegetables."

"*Puwede ninyong isigaw iyan, duktor* (You can shout that out loud, doctor)," Martin commented. "My mother-in-law would love to hear that remark."

"Does it have to be thirty days?" Mang Teroy asked disapprovingly.

"No." I answered looking at him. "In fact, it should be longer, provided they have the chickens available."

"*Araw-araw* (every day)?" he continued.

"Well, not necessarily," I answered. "she might get tired (*magsawa*) of the food."

"*Masama iyan sa family planning, duktor* (That is bad for family planning, doctor)," Mang Teroy remarked, a smile tugging at the corners of his mouth.

"How come?" I asked with evident interest. Mang Teroy knew my preoccupation with limiting and spacing of children in the barrios.

He paused for dramatic effect.

"*Pag tuwing manganganak ay manok ng manok ng tatlumpong araw, magugustuhang manganak ng palagi ng isang babae. Kung ganyan ang pagkain at palakad ay ako na ang maganak* (If every time she delivers, she is fed with chicken for thirty days, a woman will be encouraged to give birth often. If that is the feeding system and the management, I will be the one to give birth to the baby)!" Mang Teroy said with an air of wisdom and conviction.

I nodded as I listened to his reasoning. "*Mukhang may katwiran kayo*

(It looks like you have a point there)," I mused. "Next time I will tell your wife to make you carry the pregnancy."

Martin and I started laughing. Lita handed me a steaming bowl of *arroz caldo* (rice porridge with chicken broth and ginger).

"This is only for those having a baby like you," I said to Lita as the bowl was placed in my outstretched hands.

"Then give it to Tiyong Teroy," Martin commented.

"Now I know why Mang Teroy wanted to come. It is because of the arroz caldo," I said smiling.

"*Basta sumama ka sa akin, duktor, eh hindi ka magugutom* (Just go with me, doctor, and you will never go *hungry*)," Mang Teroy remarked, accepting his bowl while we all laughed.

"I might get used to (*nawiwili*) visiting you because of your arroz caldo," I said to Lita.

From Flavier, Juan M. Back to the Barrios, *Manila: New Day Publishers, 1978.*

Simbang Gabi: Mass at early dawn. Filipinos mark the coming of Christmas by going to early dawn masses starting on December 16 and culminating with midnight mass on December 24. Pen and ink by Orlando Castillo, 1986.

Recipes from the Philippines

Except in situations of the most severe poverty, whenever Filipinos gather, food is served! Filipinos usually offer visitors not only something to drink, but something to eat, however simple. A most common Filipino greeting is, "Have you eaten?" ("Kumain ka na ba?" in Pilipino.) If you are eating in front of others it is rude not to offer them some. Public places to eat, from the fanciest restaurants to the simplest sidewalk barbeque stalls, are found in the larger cities and towns, and even the smaller towns will have a great variety of eateries.

The following recipes are just a brief sampling of Filipino favorites. You might like to try them at home, or with your group at church. Combinations of these will be adequate for a complete meal, or for a snack.

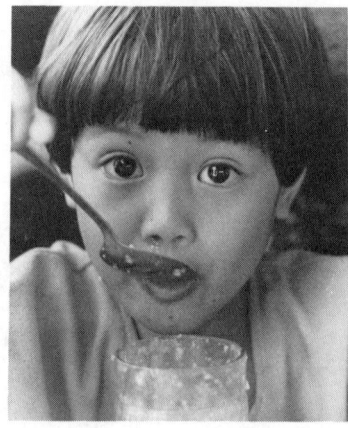

ADOBO
with chicken or pork

- 1 medium chicken or 1½ lbs. pork, cut into small serving portions
- ½ C water
- ½ C vinegar
- 2 tsp. crushed garlic (1 tsp. for stewing, 1 tsp. for browning)
- ½ tsp. salt
- 2 Tbsp. soy sauce
- 10 peppercorns
- 1 bay leaf
- 5 Tbsp. cooking fat

Stew chicken or pork in a mixture of water, vinegar, 1 tsp. garlic, salt, soy sauce, peppercorns and bay leaf. When meat is tender, remove it from the liquid and brown in hot cooking fat flavored with the remaining garlic. Add the stewing liquid to the frying pan and cook over moderate heat until sauce is thick. Serve with steamed rice. Makes 6 servings.

BIBINGKANG MALAGKIT
rice cakes made with glutinous rice

- 2 C malagkit rice (glutinous or "sticky" rice, available in food stores catering to Asians)
- 1 C brown sugar
- ¾ C rich coconut milk
- 3½ C diluted coconut milk from 2 coconuts
  (North American adaptation: Use 3/4 C thick white "cream" from the top of 2 cans of unsweetened coconut milk (available in Asian food stores) and 4 C liquid from the remainder of the 2 cans. If only sweetened coconut milk is available, reduce the amount of brown sugar by half.)
- 1 tsp. salt
- ¼ tsp. powdered anise (optional)

Bring the diluted coconut milk to boil in a wok. Add malagkit rice and salt. Simmer until quite dry, stirring constantly to keep from burning. Lower heat and add 2/3 cup brown sugar. Pour the mixture into a 9" square greased pan. Pour the rich coconut milk and the rest of the sugar on top of the rice. Sprinkle with anise seeds. Bake in 350° oven for 30 minutes. Finish off by putting under the broiler to brown the topping.

LECHE FLAN
a simplified North American version of the rich Spanish/Filipino baked milk custard

Caramelize 1/2 C sugar in a ring mold or 10" cast iron frying pan
Beat 5 eggs with
    ½ C sugar
    ¼ tsp. salt
    1 tsp. vanilla

Gradually add 3½ C milk. Set pan in another pan with 1 inch hot water. Bake at 325 degrees for 55 to 60 minutes.
For a richer custard, instead of fresh milk use one can of condensed milk and omit the sugar; or you may use 2 cans evaporated milk.

UNICEF/Jim Wright

PANCIT CANTON
a popular noodle dish originating in China

1-2 garlic cloves, crushed
1 large onion, sliced or chopped
2 carrots, sliced
1 handful of fresh green beans, cut on diagonal (french cut), or substitute sliced cabbage or broccoli spears
4 Tbsp. cooking oil
½ to 1 lb. pork, cut in small pieces
2 packages oriental noodles with chicken flavor packet (like Ramen noodles)
2 C very hot water
2-3 Tbsp. soy sauce, according to taste

Garnish with any or none of the following:

    hard-boiled egg slices
    miniature shrimp (canned or fresh)
    green pepper rings
    lemon wedges (squeezed over noodles before serving)
    chopped green onions
    fresh tomato wedges

Into a HOT wok or frying pan pour 2 Tbsp. of the oil and immediately stir in the garlic, onion and vegetables. Stir-fry until vegetables are tender but not soft. Remove vegetables to serving dish. Add remaining 2 Tbsp. oil (or fry fat trimmed from pork and use that as oil). Stir-fry pork pieces in oil until nicely browned. Add dry noodles and pour hot water over them. Gently turn with wooden spoon or fork until noodles are softened. Sprinkle packs of seasoning from noodles over meat and stir. Add vegetables and soy sauce. Stir carefully over heat and serve at once, with steamed rice. Serves 5.

CHICKEN ARROZ CALDO
a hearty chicken-rice soup

- 2 Tbsp. cooking fat
- 1 tsp. garlic
- 1 inch fresh ginger root cut into narrow strips or crushed
- 2 Tbsp. chopped onion
- 1 medium chicken, cut up (some skin may be removed)
- ½ C rice
- 5 C water
- 1 Tbsp. toasted safflower seeds (optional)
- 2 Tbsp. finely chopped green onions (scallions)
- 1 Tbsp. fried minced garlic

Saute 1 tsp. garlic, ginger, onion, chicken and rice. Add water and stir all ingredients together, making sure they do not stick to the pan. Bring to a boil, then simmer for 1 hour. Stir in safflower seeds and sprinkle with green onions and fried garlic before serving. Makes 6 servings. Great with freshly baked bread or rolls. (This may also be cooked in a crockpot.)

Games from the Philippines

Putok sa Bumbong: New year noisemaking. The new year is greeted with the sound of firecrackers. In the countryside children make "cannons" out of large bamboo pieces that explode with a large boom. Pen and ink by Orlando Castillo, 1986.

SUNGKA

In the Philippines, this game is usually played on a carved board about 2½ feet long. A North American version might use a large piece of poster board with circles drawn on it as "holes."

Goal: to get more shells or pebbles into your home than your opponent.

Setup: seven shells in each hole; no shells in home holes.

Play: In turn, players pick up all of the shells in any one of the seven holes on their own side. Then they move clockwise around the holes, dropping one shell in each hole, including their own home, but not in opponent's home.

a) If the last shell drops in a hole with shells, the player picks up all of the shells from that hole and continues to move around the board, always picking up the shells in the hole where the last shell drops, and continuing until the last shell falls in an empty hole.

b) If the last shell drops in the player's own home, player may begin another turn, picking up the shells from any hole on player's side.

c) If the last shell drops in an empty hole other than "home," the player's turn is over, but if that empty hole is on the player's own side, player gets to take the last shell, plus any shells in the opponent's hole opposite, to put in player's home. If the hole opposite has no shells, player leaves his/her own shell. If the empty hole where the last shell falls is on the opponent's side, player gets nothing to take "home."

Strategy: Always try to land on your own side, and, if possible, opposite a hole *full* of shells!

Deciding who starts: One player or the other may start, but since the first player usually gets more shells on the first turn, it is more fair (and also more confusing and challenging) if both players begin at the same time. The first player to finish the turn waits until the other is finished, then starts a second turn alone.

The end of a round: When there are no more shells for a player to start a turn, the round is over. The opponent gets the remaining shell on his/her side as a bonus.

Succeeding rounds: The players set up their holes again, with seven shells in each hole, with the extra shells "saved." If a player has insufficient shells to put seven in each of the holes, the unfilled holes are called "burned-down houses," and both players skip over those holes during that round. If a player forgets, and puts shells in a "burned-down house," the opponent may point it out and claim those shells.

End of game: Play an agreed-upon number of rounds, or until one player runs out of shells.

GROUP TAG

This active game is played in two teams with three, four or five persons on each team. The lines in the diagram are drawn on pavement with chalk or with a stick on the ground. (Indoors, masking tape can be used.)

The goal is for the players on the "offense" to run to "half-way," and then to return "home" without being tagged. If one person on the team is successful, the team gets a point and gets to try again. But if even one person gets tagged, the other team gets a turn to be the offense.

The players on the "defense" each cover their assigned line, and must keep one foot (at least a toe!) on the line.

For the players on the offense to be "safe," they must have at least one foot touching a home or half-way home line. Once inside the squares they can't go backwards, but may move from side to side. It's an advantage if they all start running at once!

The size of the square is adjustable, with the ideal layout being just large enough that the persons on the defense cannot quite cover their entire assigned area with their feet properly touching a line.

The diagram shows four players on each team. When three or five players are used, the teams will have to come to an agreement as to how to assign defensive players to the line.

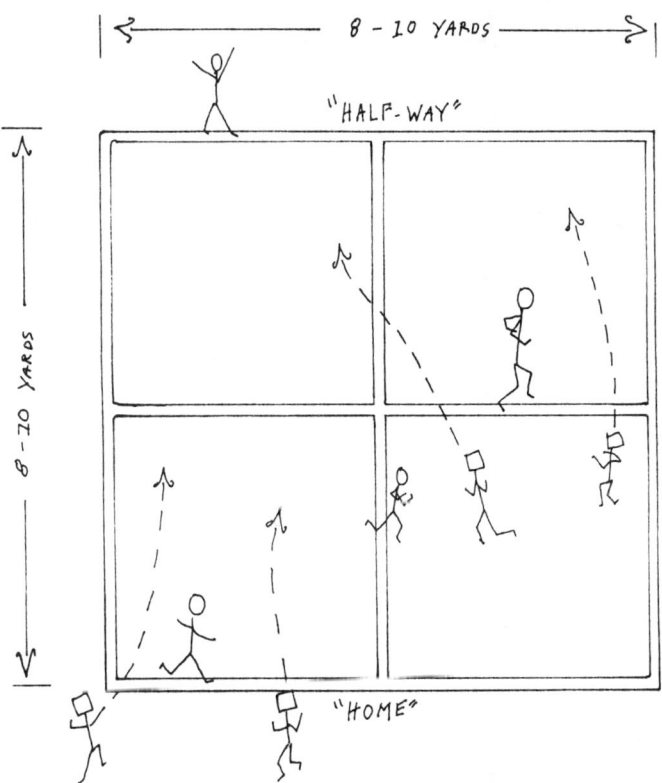

PIKO
Two versions of Filipino hopscotch

The lines are drawn with chalk on a cement surface, or are etched with a stick on the ground.

To determine the order of play, each person throws their stone towards a line diagram, to see who comes the closest.

The first person begins by tossing his or her stone into Square 1. It must land in the box, and not on the line. If there are stones in a square the players may not step in that square. If they do, they lose their turn, and if they step on a line they lose their turn.

In the second stage of the game, where players are claiming squares for their own, the players often mark their initials and decorate the squares, sometimes with very fancy designs!

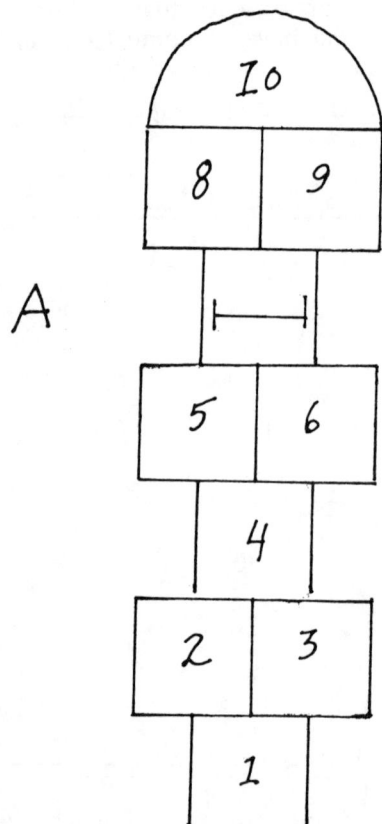

A

For Diagram A

Hop through the squares, jumping over the ones that have stones in them, including your stone. Hop on one foot for single squares, and come down on both feet when the squares are side by side. Go to Square 10 and return. On the return, stop in the square(s) just ahead of the one where your stone is, pick up your stone, and hop "home."

If you are successful, you can toss your stone into the next square, and hop through the squares again. Proceed, if possible, all the way, finally throwing your stone into Square 10. Then try it by turning your back to the squares and tossing the stone over your shoulder. At this stage, the box it lands in becomes your square, and no one else can step on that square. You start over, and try to get as many boxes for yourself as you can.

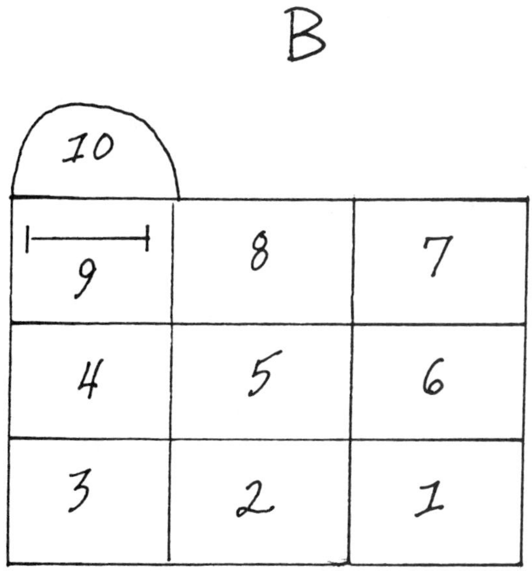

B

10		
9	8	7
4	5	6
3	2	1

For Diagram B

Toss the stone into Square 1. Hop into Square 1 and push your stone into Square 2, then Square 3, all the way up to Square 10, using your toe. You may not change legs (this gets very tiring!). Once you reach Square 10, pick up your stone and hop back home.

If your stone touches a line, or if you step on someone else's stone, you lose your turn.

If you are successful, continue by tossing your stone into Square 2. Hop into Square 1 and on to Square 2, where you start pushing your stone again with your toe.

After you make it through all 10 squares, turn your back to the squares, toss your stone over your shoulder, and the square where the stone lands becomes your own, unless someone else already has it. Try to get as many boxes as you can.

A third way of drawing the squares is in the shape of a spiral, as shown below:

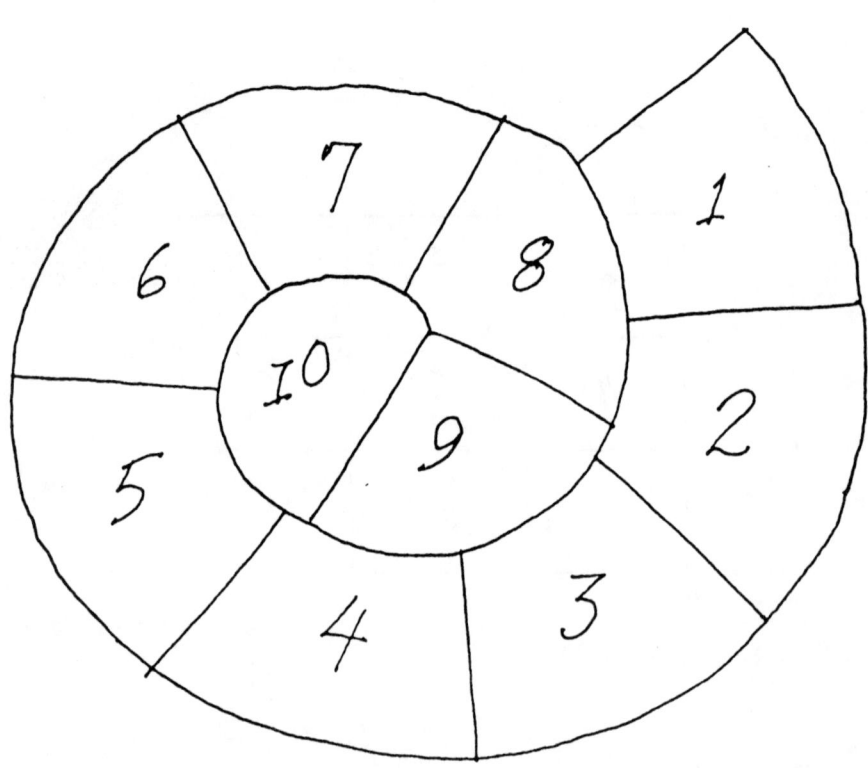

Filipinos are an attractive, gifted people. These boys are just out of the ocean; they've been diving for saltwater crabs and small fish along the reef. Note the slender fishing spear in the hand of the boy on the left.

"THONG" GAME

Here is a game that children in the Philippines play using their ordinary rubber thongs.

Stand behind the line and try to throw one of your thongs into the circle. If you miss, you lose your turn. If it gets in, hop toward the circle on one foot, with the other thong balanced in top of your other foot. If you drop it, you lose your turn. Once you reach the circle, let the thong you are balancing fall to touch the thong in the circle. If you miss, you lose your turn. If it touches, pick it up, return it to its balanced position (while remaining on one foot), and hop back to the line, leaving the other thong in the circle. Continue, using other balancing positions as agreed upon. Some ideas: in palm of hand; on back of hand; on top of head; squeezed behind the knee, etc. Give points as agreed, with more points for the more difficult positions.

RUBBER BAND GAMES

Blowing rubber bands

Blow your rubber band in your opponent's direction. The goal is to get your rubber band to overlap the other person's rubber band. If you're successful, their rubber band becomes your property.

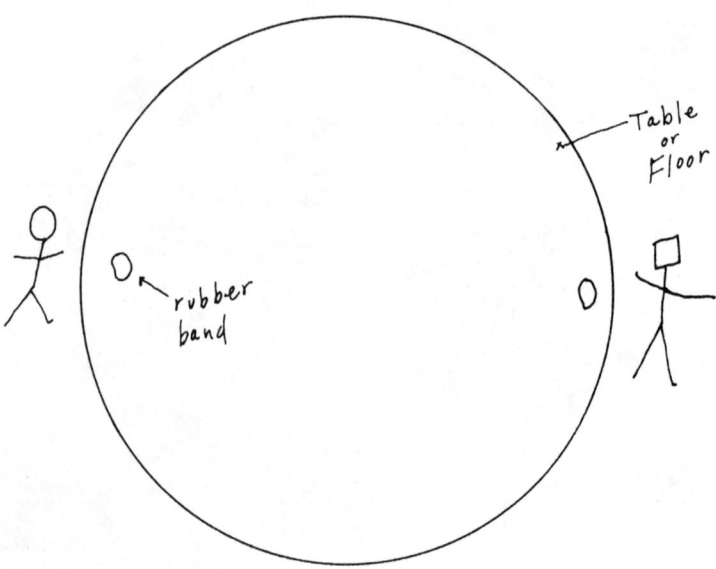

"Loose" the rubber bands

Each player puts rubber bands together in a kind of figure eight position (see diagram: not too tightly) in singles, or doubles, or triples (the more the rubber bands, the easier they are to loosen). Taking turns, try to get the rubber bands loose by snapping at them (one "snap" per turn) — flicking your index finger off your thumb. The rubber bands that come loose become the property of the one who caused it. A variation is to kick them with the toe.

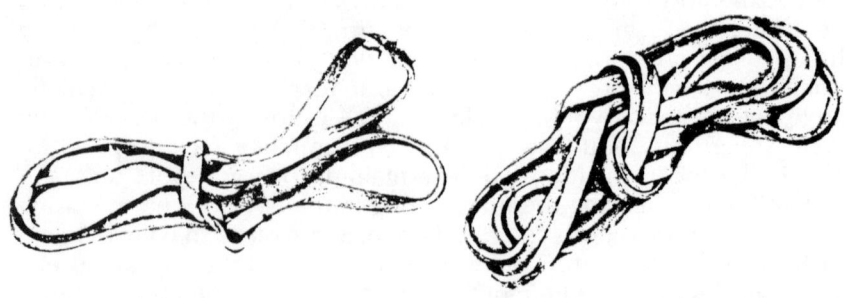

Throw into the circle

Each player throws the same agreed-upon number of rubber bands into a circle in a pile. In turn, players stand behind a line which is at an agreed-upon distance from the circle, either tossing or "shooting" a rubber band at the pile. Any rubber bands that theirs overlaps become their property.

B. David Williams

Rubber band high jump

Prepare a simple rope by stringing rubber bands together in any of the various ways shown in the diagram. With a player holding each end, let the other players, in turn, jump over it, starting with the rope on the ground, and then going progressively higher. Go as high as you can. The one who can jump the highest wins. No prize, just the admiration of others!

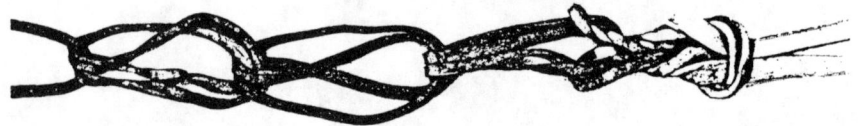

Rubber band jump rope

Three or more persons can play in turn. Make a chain of rubber bands in a loop. Two people stand in the loop, far enough apart so that the rubber bands don't sag. With the loop at the level of the ankles, a jumper begins on one side of the bands and jumps in the following sequence: (1) in, (2) out, (3) left band between legs, (4) right band between legs, (5) jump and land with the two bands trapped under the feet (it's easier if you're barefoot!), (6) in again, (7) then back to starting position. The diagram shows where your feet should land after each jump.

If the jumper is successful, he or she progresses to "calves"—with the loop of rubber bands held halfway between the ankle and knee. Then knees, then thighs, then hips, waist, armpits, shoulders, and neck (for experts). When the jumper makes a mistake, he or she must hold the rope while the next person jumps. At the next turn, the jumper begins with the level previously not completed.

Sequence for jumping:
   start
   1. "in"
   2. "out"
   3. "side"
   4. "to side"
   5. "on"
   6. "in"
   7. "out"

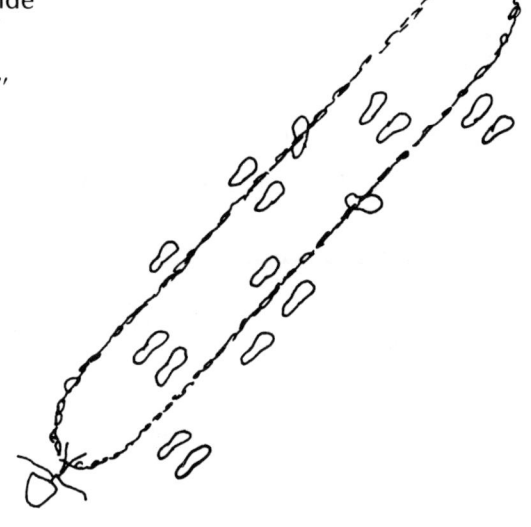

Positions for loop:
   ankles
   calves
   knees
   thighs
   hips
   waist
   armpits
   neck (spread rubber bands with hands to give room for jumper)

Thanks to Karen Wehrman Graves, Esther Wehrman Otero, and Denise Williams, former "missionary kids" in the Philippines, who have helped in identifying and explaining these games.

Some Tagalog Proverbs

For help in pronunciation, see Glossary in Rice in the Storm.

Tubig mang matahimik maaaring magkabuwaya.
 Even still waters may contain crocodiles.

Malakas ang bulong sa sigaw.
 A whisper may sometimes seem louder than a shout.

Taong nagigipit, sa patalim ma'y kakapit.
 A man falling from the ledge will grab even the razor's edge.

Mamatay sa gutom na nakalalaya'y mabuting higit sa aliping mataba.
 It is better to be hungry but free than to be a fat slave.

Magdamit hari man kung talagang hangal mahahalata rin sa kilos at asal.
 You may hide behind a nice dress, but your behavior will undress your true self.

Walang utang na di pinagbayaran.
 There is no such thing as a debt that was not paid for somehow.

Walang pagod sa pagtipon, walang sayang sa pagtapon.
 Easy come, easy go.

Ang sakit ng kalingkingan damdamin ng buong katawan.
 Pain in the small finger is felt all over.

Madali pang gisingin ang tulog na nahihimbing kay sa iyong pukawin iyong talaga namang gising.
 It is easier to wake one who is in deep slumber than one who is awake but pretends to be in slumber.

Aanhin pa ang damo kung patay na ang kabayo.
 Of what use is hay, if the horse is already dead.

Mahirap ang umakyat, masarap ang nasa itaas.
 It is difficult to climb, but it feels good to be at the top.

A Philippine Quiz

Mark statements "True" or "False." Find answers by reading Rice in the Storm.

1. Manila's University of Santo Tomas is older than Harvard University.

2. Christians are a minority in the Philippines.

3. Prices in general retail businesses, such as public markets, are fixed, and one should never haggle.

4. When commemorating the anniversary of the dead on All Saints Day, it is not proper to bring food and eat near the tombstones.

5. The Philippines "exports" more nurses than any other nation.

6. Office workers consider afternoon tea, or *merienda*, an institution that enhances the quality of the work.

7. The Philippines "exports" more doctors than any other nation.

8. Three out of ten Filipino children become malnourished before they reach the age of five, and only four in ten grow up to be healthy.

9. The Philippines consists of 5,000 islands.

10. The infant mortality rate is lower in the rural areas than in the metro Manila area.

ANSWERS:

1. True. The University of Sto. Tomas was founded in 1611.
2. False. Well over 90 percent of the people identify themselves as Christians.
3. False: It is considered quite proper to bargain, although in many of the department stores in cities the prices are fixed.
4. False: Food is always a part of the great family celebrations of loved ones at the cemeteries on November 1.
5. True.
6. True.
7. False: India does. The Philippines is second.
8. True (Feb. 1986 report of Health Minister Azurin to UNICEF)
9. False: more than 7,100.
10. False: it is usually two to four times as high, depending upon the area (National Census and Statistics Office).

Some Filipino Riddles

(selections from the 1986 Philippine Almanac)

1. Which fruit has its seed outside?
2. Sky overhead, sky underneath, water in the middle.
3. A house on a molehill with only one post.
4. It has many eyes but cannot see.
5. What animal is born twice?
6. When it stands, it is small; when it sits, it is tall.
7. How does a dry fish eat?
8. What are twins but do not know nor see each other?
9. If it is full, it stands; hungry, it collapses.
10. What fish is that whose body is here but whose head is in America?
11. What has one eye but cannot see?
12. What has one entrance and three exits?
13. What has a tongue but cannot talk?
14. The more you keep it alive, the shorter its life; the more you put it out, the longer its life.
15. What "santa" (saint) has four legs?
16. When not seen, carried; when seen, killed.
17. What starts like a submarine swimming, then ends like an airplane, stinging?
18. Separated at daytime; close friends at nightime.
19. Who cannot tell a lie, nor leave any footprints?
20. What is it that spreads into branches but has neither fruits nor leaves?

ANSWERS:

1. the cashew 2. a coconut 3. mushroom 4. pineapple 5. chicken 6. dog 7. a dried fish doesn't eat! 8. the ears 9. a sack 10. canned salmon 11. a needle 12. an undershirt 13. a shoe 14. a candle 15. santa mesa (which means "holy table" in Spanish) 16. lice 17. a mosquito 18. the eyelids 19. a corpse 20. a deer's antlers